Ladders

WELCOME TO
BRAZIL
AROUND THE WORLD

Into the Rain Forest

by David Holford

Brazil is the largest country in South America. Half of Brazil is covered by the Amazon **rain forest**. Rain forests are warm and wet. They have many kinds of animals and plants. It rains almost every day in the rain forest.

Brazil's rain forest gets its name from the Amazon River. This river winds through the forest for many miles.

The Amazon rain forest is home to strange fish. The electric eel is a fish that looks like a snake. It can zap its enemies with electric shocks!

More types of plants and animals live in the Amazon rain forest than anywhere else in the world. Most of the animals live in the **canopy**. The canopy is made up of branches and leaves. It is found at the top of the forest. Chattering monkeys, colorful

A Home in the Forest

Many **tribes** live in the Amazon rain forest. Tribes are groups of people with the same language and beliefs. One of these tribes is the Yanomami (yah-noh-MAH-mee).

The Yanomami live in villages. Several families live together in large, round houses. The houses are made with vines and leaves. The men and older boys hunt monkeys, birds, and other animals for food. They use bows and poison arrows.

The Yanomami also grow food in gardens. The men chop down trees and other plants. Then they set the cuttings on fire. This burning clears land to make room for gardens.

After the burning, the women plant and tend the crops. Their work is hard but important. Much of the tribe's food comes from gardens.

∨ This Yanomami girl wears flowers and paints her face for a celebration.

∨ Instead of a cat or a dog, this young Yanomami man keeps two parrots as pets.

This boy picked these bananas from a tree. The feathers on his head are from a parrot. The Yanomami get everything they need to live from the rain forest.

Squirrel Monkey

Red-and-Green Macaw

Green Anaconda Snake

Three-Toed Sloth

Giant Anteater

Pink River Dolphin

6

Respect the Rain Forest

The Yanomami treat the Amazon rain forest well. The forest has things they need to live. They use plants and animals for food, clothing, and building homes. But the Yanomami take only what they need to stay alive. They know that taking more than they need would hurt the rain forest.

Many Brazilians work hard to protect the rain forest from people who cut it down. Cutting down trees hurts the homes of animals. It also wastes useful plants that grow in the rain forest. Some plants are usedto make medicines that save lives.

People on vacation visit the Amazon rain forest. They enjoy seeing the tall trees and colorful animals. They can protect the forest by leaving no trace of their visit.

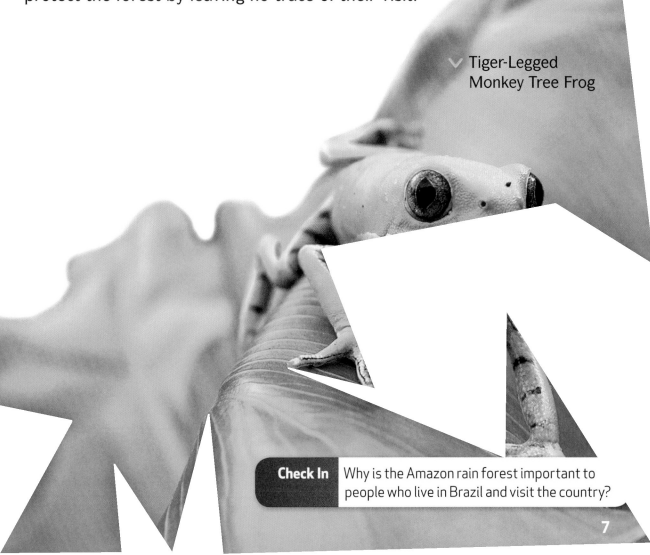

˅ Tiger-Legged Monkey Tree Frog

Check In Why is the Amazon rain forest important to people who live in Brazil and visit the country?

Let's Go to Carnival!

by Hugh Westrup

> During each day of Carnival, more than 2 million people gather in the streets to celebrate. That's one big party!

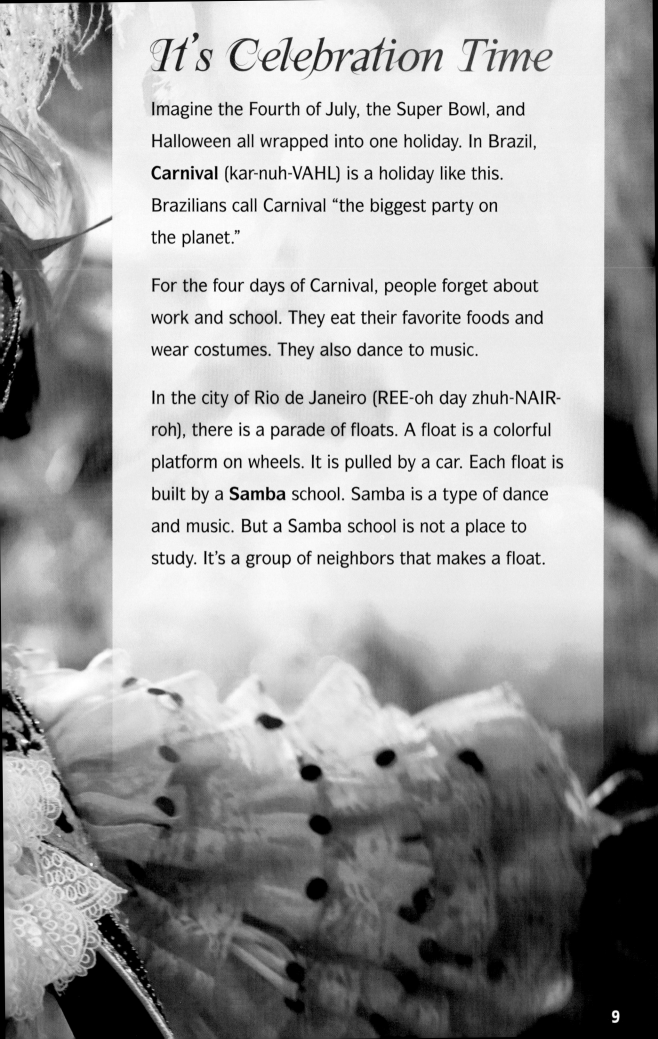

It's Celebration Time

Imagine the Fourth of July, the Super Bowl, and Halloween all wrapped into one holiday. In Brazil, **Carnival** (kar-nuh-VAHL) is a holiday like this. Brazilians call Carnival "the biggest party on the planet."

For the four days of Carnival, people forget about work and school. They eat their favorite foods and wear costumes. They also dance to music.

In the city of Rio de Janeiro (REE-oh day zhuh-NAIR-roh), there is a parade of floats. A float is a colorful platform on wheels. It is pulled by a car. Each float is built by a **Samba** school. Samba is a type of dance and music. But a Samba school is not a place to study. It's a group of neighbors that makes a float.

> People spend thousands of hours painting a float. They use just as many gallons of paint.

∧ A man makes a big flower for a float. This flower makes up one small part of a huge float.

It's a good thing grasshoppers aren't this big in real life!

Top-Secret Floats

Samba schools work hard to get ready for Carnival. Each Samba school has a **theme** for its float. A theme is a big idea. Everything on the float relates to that theme. One theme might be about the Amazon rain forest.

Floats are very big. They are put together inside huge buildings. Many people work together to build a float. For a float about the rain forest, builders might make a large riverboat. Artists might make animals out of cloth and wire. Flowers might be made out of paper and glue. Everything about the float is kept secret until Carnival. Each Samba school wants its float to be a surprise!

Get Up and Dance!

Samba music has fast drumbeats and loud horns. When you hear Samba music, you just have to dance! Each Samba school plays a new song every year. The dancers dance to this song during the parades. Before Carnival, the dancers practice a long time.

Many people make costumes for Carnival dancers and musicians. Every outfit is made by hand. Miles of cloth, thousands of feathers, and millions of sparkling decorations are used for making the costumes.

The colors of the costumes are very bright. Red, yellow, pink, and blue are some of the colors that are used. But the costumes must be cool to wear. Carnival is held in February or March. That is the warmest time of the year in Brazil.

< This woman is called the "Queen of Drums." She leads the drummers in the parade.

^ Dancers perform in groups called *wings*. Each wing has as many as 100 dancers. Everyone in the wing wears the same costume.

A float makes its way through a cheering crowd in the Sambadrome. Forty judges decide which float is the best.

Parade Time

Samba schools show off their hard work in a place called the **Sambadrome**. This big building is like an outdoor stage. A long road stretches down the middle. The judges and crowds sit on both sides of the road. As each school enters the Sambadrome, the crowd cheers.

On the last two nights of Carnival, the 12 best Samba schools perform. Each school plays and dances for the judges. First, the school's flag is carried into the Sambadrome. Next, the drummers enter. Then the dancers twirl to the music. They look like colorful birds.

Finally, the floats enter the Sambadrome. The crowd goes wild. Only one Samba school can win the float contest. No matter which school wins, the people of Rio de Janeiro have put on a great show!

Check In How does a community work together during Carnival?

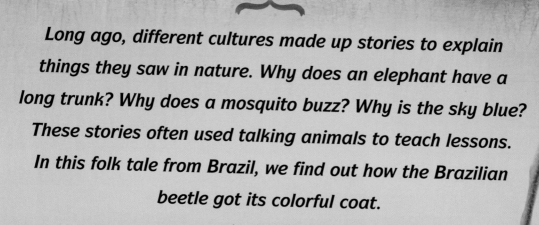

How Beetle Got Her Coat

retold by Jenny Loomis

illustrated by Cecilia Rébora

Long ago, different cultures made up stories to explain things they saw in nature. Why does an elephant have a long trunk? Why does a mosquito buzz? Why is the sky blue? These stories often used talking animals to teach lessons. In this folk tale from Brazil, we find out how the Brazilian beetle got its colorful coat.

One hot afternoon, Beetle took a stroll through the rain forest. She loved to look at the orchids (AWR-kihdz) after the morning rains had stopped. As she walked along a dirt path, she smiled at the beautiful colors of the flowers. Their petals came in every shade of the rainbow. She really liked the shiny blues and deep lime greens. Beetle looked at her own dull brown coat. She sighed, "If only my coat was as colorful as the orchids."

Suddenly, Beetle heard splashing in the river. She turned to see Rat swimming toward her. He jumped out of the water and said, "Poor Beetle! How slowly you walk! It must take you forever to get anything done. Too bad you aren't more like me. I move so fast I'll make your head spin!"

Beetle rolled her eyes and kept walking. It was best to ignore Rat when he started bragging.

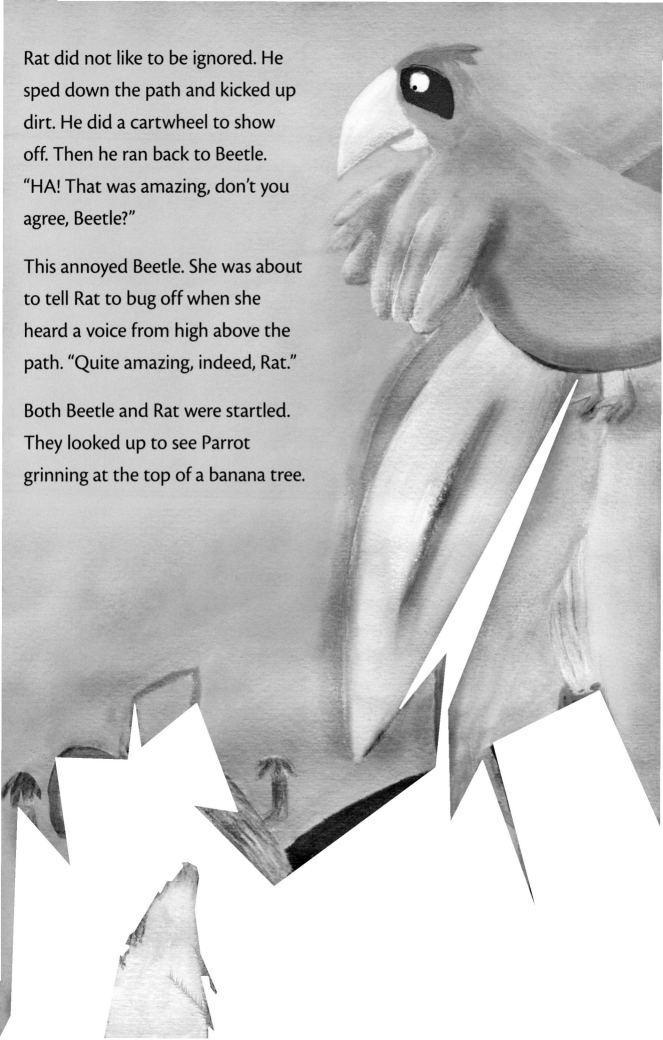

Rat did not like to be ignored. He sped down the path and kicked up dirt. He did a cartwheel to show off. Then he ran back to Beetle. "HA! That was amazing, don't you agree, Beetle?"

This annoyed Beetle. She was about to tell Rat to bug off when she heard a voice from high above the path. "Quite amazing, indeed, Rat."

Both Beetle and Rat were startled. They looked up to see Parrot grinning at the top of a banana tree.

"Your speed gives me an idea for a race. The prize will be a beautiful coat in any color the winner likes. Interested?" asked Parrot.

Rat jumped with excitement. "This is great! I'm finally going to have a shiny black coat! No one notices how fast I am because my brown and white coat is so boring. Once I get a black coat, the other animals will give me more attention. Let's start this race," squeaked Rat.

The thought of a new colorful coat made Beetle happy. She also agreed to the race.

"The first animal to reach that large nut tree wins. Ready?
GO!" yelled Parrot.

Rat ran without looking back. He kept thinking about
how handsome he would look in his new black coat. He
danced happily when he got to the tree. Looking around
for Parrot, Rat announced, "I won, Parrot! I want my shiny
black coat now!"

Rat looked up at the nut tree. He couldn't believe what he saw. Sitting next to Parrot was Beetle. Beetle was wearing a sparkling blue and green coat.

"How did you get here so fast, Beetle? I didn't see you pass me," asked Rat angrily.

"I flew up here," replied Beetle.

"Flew? I didn't know you could fly!" yelled Rat.

"Rat, you don't know anything about me. You only talk to me when you make fun of me," explained Beetle. "You thought I was slow and weak. You were wrong."

Rat was angry. He kicked the nut tree, shaking a Brazil nut loose. It fell on his head.

From that day on, Beetle proudly wore her fancy blue and green coat in the rain forest. She was as colorful as the orchids that she loved.

Rat had his same old coat, but he changed in other ways. He stopped judging the other animals by how they looked. Rat knew he might end up racing one of them some day!

Check In Why did Rat think that Beetle could not win the race?

Discuss

1. What connections can you make among the three selections that you read in this book?

2. In what ways do the Yanomami people depend on the Amazon rain forest? What could happen to their way of life if the rain forest is not protected?

3. Tell about the tradition of Carnival in Brazil. Describe how a tradition in your country is similar to Carnival.

4. Folk tales often use animals to teach lessons about how to behave. What lessons did you learn by reading this folk tale?

5. What do you still wonder about life in Brazil?